IMAGES
of America

HARPERS FERRY
NATIONAL HISTORICAL PARK

Park ranger Adam Craven assists in guiding a tour of young people from Washington, DC, as part of the 1960s "Project Catch-Up." The park is the perfect place to explore issues of leadership, character, equality, and fairness through the prism of history. Above the group is a sign calling attention to exhibits pertaining to abolitionist John Brown. (Courtesy of National Park Service; photograph by Andrew Hutchinson.)

ON THE COVER: Taken in June 1961 by photographer Jack Boucher, this image captures a park ranger surveying the view of the town of Harpers Ferry and the park below. This gorgeous sweeping vista also encompasses the confluence of two of America's most storied great rivers. The Shenandoah River, flowing in from the left, merges with the Potomac River, coming in from the right-hand side of this photograph. (Courtesy of National Park Service.)

IMAGES
of America

HARPERS FERRY
NATIONAL HISTORICAL PARK

James A. Beckman

ARCADIA
PUBLISHING

Published by Arcadia Publishing
Charleston, South Carolina

Library of Congress Control Number: 2020933866

For all general information, please contact Arcadia Publishing:
Telephone 843-853-2070
Fax 843-853-0044
E-mail sales@arcadiapublishing.com
For customer service and orders:
Toll-Free 1-888-313-2665

Visit us on the Internet at www.arcadiapublishing.com

*To all park employees and volunteers, past and present,
who selflessly and tirelessly worked to preserve the jewel
that is Harpers Ferry National Historical Park*

CONTENTS

Acknowledgments

Books rarely come into existence based on the author's own devices and work alone. As such, I am indebted to many individuals, named and unnamed, who were instrumental in playing a role in this book.

I extend my thanks to all Arcadia employees who had a role in making this a better book. Specifically, I would like to thank two individuals, Katelyn Jenkins and Caitrin Cunningham. Katelyn Jenkins, acquisitions editor, recognized the value of a book of this nature and reached out to me to see if I would be willing to undertake another book for Arcadia. Katelyn offered sound advice on constructing a strong book proposal and ushering the proposal through the Arcadia approval process. Caitrin Cunningham, senior title manager, served as my editor for this book. I could not imagine a better editor, and I thank her for her many acts of kindness and guidance.

I would like to acknowledge the support of Dr. Alisa Smith, my department chair at the University of Central Florida, who not only allows me the intellectual autonomy to pursue research and publication topics for which I feel most passionate but also encourages me to do so.

I am particularly grateful for the support, expertise, and friendship of Catherine Baldau, executive director, Harpers Ferry Park Association. She graciously agreed to review the text and page proofs for this book despite her extraordinarily busy schedule. Also, I want to thank Ranger Michael Hosking for pulling multiple binders of unprocessed images and allowing me to review and scan pertinent photographs for this book. And thanks go to David Larsen and Susan Journell, who introduced me and my wife to many of the intriguing stories and history of the park; much of our early knowledge and burgeoning love of the park we owe to them.

Last, but not least, I thank my wife, Maria Beckman. She provided a critical eye on the suitability of certain images, reviewed text, and provided all-around support. I am indebted to her not just for help on this book but also for being an indispensable part of my life and a wonderful life partner.

INTRODUCTION

The Harpers Ferry National Historical Park (hereinafter, the "park") is a truly amazing place and one of the jewels of the US National Park System. First as a national monument, the park was established by congressional legislation during the trying days of World War II and signed into law by Pres. Franklin D. Roosevelt in 1944. In 1963, Pres. John F. Kennedy signed into law legislation that elevated Harpers Ferry from the status of a national monument to a national historical park.

Compared with its initial size of no land in 1944 and only 515 acres eight years after its establishment as a park, the present-day park encompasses over 3,660 acres and not only spans thousands of acres of historical trails, Civil War battlefields, landmarks, and dozens of historically significant structures but also spans three different states (West Virginia, Virginia, and Maryland) and includes the confluence of the Shenandoah and Potomac Rivers. As a certified guide for the Harpers Ferry Park Association, I am frequently asked by visitors why the park is so large in terms of acreage or what exactly happened in and around Harpers Ferry to merit such a large park. In answering these questions for visitors and for the readers of this book, a brief recitation of some of the town's most compelling historic events is required.

The town of Harpers Ferry was a famous tourist destination over 150 years before the federal government established a national monument. On October 25, 1783, future president Thomas Jefferson visited the area and wrote his memorable observations of his visit for posterity. Jefferson eloquently remarked that the scenery was "perhaps one of the most stupendous scenes in nature" and the "scene is worth a voyage across the Atlantic." Jefferson's praise of the area was published in papers around the globe and also appeared in his book titled *Notes on the State of Virginia*, prompting the first generation of tourists that would mushroom to throngs of Americans in the ensuing centuries.

George Washington was another of the famous visitors to Harpers Ferry, and he visited often. Washington's first visit was as a member of Lord Fairfax's surveying expedition when he was 16. He visited often in the 1780s as president of the Patowmack Canal Company. Washington's visits and observation of the resources of the area inspired him to order the establishment of the federal armory and arsenal at Harpers Ferry in 1794. In fact, Washington wrote that "this spot affords every advantage . . . and that no place is more capable of complete defense at small offense."

By 1861, the Harpers Ferry Armory would produce approximately 600,000 muskets and rifles. These muskets and rifles produced at the armory were used by Capt. Meriwether Lewis and his men in the Lewis and Clark Expedition in 1803–1806, as well as in the War of 1812, the Mexican-American War, and the Civil War. As the armory blossomed into a major industrial site, a prosperous town concurrently developed around the armory. The prosperity of the town and the operation of the US Armory and Arsenal necessitated an appropriate transportation infrastructure. By the 1830s, Harpers Ferry was at the cutting edge of the transportation revolution that soon would sweep the nation. The Chesapeake & Ohio Canal reached the town on the opposite shoreline in 1832, and the Baltimore & Ohio Railroad arrived a year later. By 1836, the

Winchester & Potomac Railroad was completed, connecting Harpers Ferry with Winchester, Virginia. By 1837, the Baltimore & Ohio Railroad completed a major bridge across the confluence of the Shenandoah and Potomac Rivers. The railroad bridge over the confluence also connected the Baltimore & Ohio to the Winchester & Potomac line. This was a time of great industry, construction, and innovation in Harpers Ferry.

Perhaps most well-known is the fact that Harpers Ferry was the epicenter of radical abolitionist John Brown's attempt in 1859 to seize the US Armory at Harpers Ferry, liberate the local enslaved population, and foment a slave rebellion throughout the South. On October 18, 1859, Brown was ultimately captured by 90 US Marines, led by Lt. Col. Robert E. Lee. Of the 21 men in Brown's "Army of Liberation," 10 would be killed during the raid of the town and 7 would be executed in the months following the raid. Brown himself was executed on December 2, 1859. A mere 18 months after Brown's attempted slave insurrection, the town of Harpers Ferry became a highly sought after prize of war between the contending armies, and the town was of immense strategic value. Among other confrontations that took place in town during the Civil War, the Siege of Harpers Ferry directly preceded the Battle of Antietam in September 1862. One of the results of this siege was that a garrison of 12,400 Union soldiers surrendered to Confederate forces. This would be the largest surrender of US troops until the Battle of Bataan in 1942. Two weeks after the Siege of Harpers Ferry, no less an important figure than Pres. Abraham Lincoln visited the town to inspect the Union Army of the Potomac then occupying the town.

During and after the Civil War, the town became a refuge for African Americans. During the war, thousands upon thousands of African Americans fled the South and sought protection of the Union army at Harpers Ferry. After the war, the establishment of Storer College in 1867 brought African American students, staff, and faculty from around the country. The town was also the meeting place for veterans' reunions, the annual Baltimore & Ohio Railroad company picnic, and civil rights organizations, including the Niagara Movement meetings in 1906.

As one might imagine, there have been hundreds of books referencing the various historical events that took place in Harpers Ferry from the town's founding in 1747 until the early 20th century. However, only a small handful of books have focused primarily on the history of the national park itself in Harpers Ferry. In June 2019, the park commemorated its 75th anniversary, and the event was marked by speakers, presentations, tours, musical performances, and other activities. In light of the general paucity of books on the park itself and in continued celebration of the park's 75th, this book project was undertaken.

This book celebrates the founding, establishment, and growth of the park. The book not only depicts how the park came to be established but also the hard and sometimes controversial decisions that often had to be made along the way in deciding what needed to be preserved and why. The book also depicts and celebrates the hard work and dedication of thousands of park employees and volunteers over the years and decades in stabilizing, restoring, preserving, and interpreting the park resources for future generations of Americans. As I wrote in a previous book on Harpers Ferry, "the history of Harpers Ferry is America's history—to be treasured and enjoyed by all who visit." Likewise, the history of the park constitutes part of the fabric and heritage of not only the National Park Service but also all visitors. The history of the park should also be treasured and enjoyed and appreciated by all who visit.

Several final notes on the ensuing pages of this book. In researching and preparing this book, I reviewed upwards of 6,000 images of the park. Unfortunately, only a small fraction of those images can be presented here, and subjective decisions were made on what photographs best represented a certain event. Similarly, as the park covers thousands of acres and includes hundreds of historic buildings, structures, and landmarks, it is impossible to depict and discuss everything in this book. Of course, not every building in the park is chronicled. Likewise, it was impossible to name and highlight the countless contributions of thousands of individuals who have come through the park in the course of the last 75 years. As such, calculated decisions were made as to what images would best tell the pictorial history of the park and inspire the reader to conduct additional independent reading and research. The goal in designing this book was that the history of the national park at Harpers Ferry would be sequentially told from moving from image to image and image caption to image caption. The intention is that one photograph relates to the next photograph, and the reader can visually see the history of the park unfold by moving from image to image throughout the subsequent pages of this book.

Lastly, a great majority of the images comes from either the National Park Service or the Library of Congress. As it relates to the National Park Service, unless otherwise noted in the book, the photographs more specifically originated from either the National Park Service Harpers Ferry Modern Photo Collection or the Harpers Ferry Unprocessed Collection. Every effort was made to be as detailed and correct as possible in the captions and in the image credits. Of course, to err is human, and if mistakes were made, such mistakes were assuredly unintentional and regrettable. Any mistakes with the text, captions, or image credits are the author's own.

One

WHY HARPERS FERRY?

In this 1860s Currier & Ives lithograph, two men on horseback are depicted with the confluence of the Potomac and Shenandoah Rivers in the background. Immediately above the Potomac River and to the right of the confluence of the two rivers is the town of Harpers Ferry. The town, founded in 1747, is depicted here in its infancy. (Courtesy of Library of Congress.)

Thomas Jefferson made this rock formation famous when he claimed that the view from this location was "worth a voyage across the Atlantic" to see. On October 25, 1783, the future president of the United States visited Harpers Ferry and surveyed the rugged, untouched beauty of this part of Virginia. Jefferson wrote that "you stand on a very high point of land; on your right comes up the Shenandoah, having ranged along the foot of the mountains a hundred miles to find a vent; on your left approaches the Potomac, in quest of a passage also. In the moment of their junction, they push together against the mountain, rend it asunder, and pass off to the sea. The scene is worth a voyage across the Atlantic." Jefferson's Rock is a major feature within the park today, and people have visited this location for hundreds of years, including other presidents (such as John Quincy Adams in 1834 and Bill Clinton in 1998). (Courtesy of Library of Congress.)

In 1794, Pres. George Washington selected Harpers Ferry, Virginia, to be the site of one of the two national armories. By December 1799, the first armory paymaster reported to his superiors in the War Department that "the Arsenal is built but not entirely finished. Two upper floors are yet to be laid . . . [the] arsenal has three floors . . . [and] stands within the confluence" of the Potomac and Shenandoah Rivers. This engraving, dating from the early 1800s, is the earliest known depiction of that building. Visiting the park today, the location of the arsenal building can be found in Arsenal Square in the town's historical center (called "Lower Town"). While the arsenal building was destroyed during the Civil War, the boundaries of the building are marked out by the park for visitors today. Arsenal Square was the site of archaeological digs by the park on several occasions, and artifacts found in those digs are on display in the park. (Courtesy of Library of Congress.)

Virginius Island was incorporated in 1827. Depicted here in 1857, the island had over 40 privately owned businesses, the US Armory Rifle Factory complex (Hall's Rifle Works), and approximately 200 residents. The four-story building located at the top left of this lithograph was the cotton mill. The cotton mill was erected in 1847 and served as a hospital for soldiers during the Civil War. The buildings of this once-thriving island finally disappeared after the devastating flood of 1936, and the island was reclaimed by nature. Today, park visitors may take a 1.5-mile nature walk around the island. Foundations of several of the buildings may still be found as one walks around the island. The foundations of the cotton mill are very well preserved and can be seen as soon as one crosses the pedestrian bridge and enters onto Virginius Island. (Courtesy of National Park Service.)

The preserved town center of the park, called "Lower Town," is depicted in this 1850s print. The Shenandoah River (left) and Potomac River (right) merge at the point of the old covered bridge (center). The conglomeration of buildings just across the confluence constitutes Lower Town. The old US Armory complex is depicted along the banks of the Potomac River adjacent to Lower Town and to the right of Lower Town in this print. The knoll, or hill, above Lower Town is the Camp Hill section of town, which earned its name because approximately one fourth of the American standing army in 1799 was stationed in Harpers Ferry and bivouacked up on the hill. Completed in 1836, the bridge traversing the confluence allowed for the Baltimore & Ohio to enter through the town and also to be connected with the Winchester & Potomac line. The Chesapeake & Ohio Canal reached Harpers Ferry in 1832 and can be seen on the right bottom corner of this print. (Courtesy of Library of Congress.)

This 1885 photograph shows the armory fire engine house used by John Brown during his attempted seizure of the armory and arsenal in October 1859. The building was subsequently painted with "John Brown's Fort" to attract tourists aboard the passing trains. Excluding buildings used by armory officials as residences, John Brown's Fort is the only extant armory complex building still standing within the park today. (Courtesy of Library of Congress.)

This engraving was published in *Frank Leslie's Illustrated Newspaper* on October 29, 1859, and depicts the moment the US Marines stormed the fire engine house in order to capture John Brown on October 18, 1859. John Brown's Fort is one of the important landmarks in the park and is located today in the old Arsenal Square grounds. (Courtesy of Library of Congress.)

The arsenal at Harpers Ferry is shown in flames as loyal Southern citizens carry away to safety the munitions and equipment stored in the building. The small detachment of Federal guards, unable to stop the larger Virginia militia, had set fire to the armory and arsenal on April 18, 1861, in the hopes of destroying everything. This event occurred 24 hours after Virginia voted to secede. (Courtesy of Library of Congress.)

During the Civil War, the town changed hands eight times, four times held by Southern armies and four times by Northern armies. By war's end, North and South combined, hundreds of thousands of soldiers were stationed or moved through Harpers Ferry. Buildings utilized by these soldiers can be seen throughout the park today. This 1862 photograph captures members of the 22nd New York State Militia. (Courtesy of Library of Congress.)

Many significant military engagements took place in and around the town, the most significant being the Siege of Harpers Ferry, which involved approximately 23,000 Southern soldiers against a Union garrison of 15,000. The Union would surrender 12,400 men at the end of this siege, and this constituted the largest surrender of US troops until 1942. The various battlefields are preserved and part of the park. (Courtesy of Library of Congress.)

Multiple presidents have visited Harpers Ferry. Prior to the park's creation, some notable visits included those by George Washington, Thomas Jefferson, James Madison, John Quincy Adams, Abraham Lincoln, Ulysses Grant, Woodrow Wilson, and Franklin D. Roosevelt. After the park's creation, US presidents Jimmy Carter and Bill Clinton visited the park. Lincoln (tallest person pictured) posed for this photograph at Antietam on October 3, 1862, just a day after visiting Harpers Ferry. (Courtesy of Library of Congress.)

One Civil War soldier remarked that while the town had once been grand, "the entire place is not now worth even $10." This photograph was taken immediately after the Confederates abandoned the town in June 1861—only three months after Virginia seceded. Compare this image with the image on page 15 and note the damage already wrought on the town. (Courtesy of Library of Congress.)

This 1865 photograph shows some of the damage to the town during the Civil War. Many of the buildings that existed in Lower Town were damaged or destroyed. Across the Potomac River (left) is Maryland Heights, Maryland, and across the Shenandoah River (right) is Loudoun Heights, Virginia. Both Maryland Heights and Loudoun Heights are contained within the boundaries of the park today. (Courtesy of Library of Congress.)

THE SHENANDOAH

B. & O. R. R. BRIDGE

This 1906 panoramic postcard depicts the town of Harpers Ferry as it looked in the late 1800s and early 1900s. The photograph used to create this postcard was taken from atop Maryland Heights, which looms approximately 1,600 feet above the town below. From this view, minus Maryland Heights itself, one can see much of what encompasses Harpers Ferry National Historical Park today. On the left-hand side, Loudoun Heights can be seen. A couple hundred acres of the park are located on Loudoun Heights. Across the confluence sits the town of Harpers Ferry. The town is a

THE POTOMAC.

COPYRIGHT 1906
W. E. DITTMEYER
HARPERS FERRY, W.VA.

ARPER'S FERRY, W.VA., FROM MARYLAND HEIGHTS

peninsula, a tongue-shaped piece of land enveloped by the Shenandoah River (left) and Potomac River (right). The flat stretch of barren land running along the banks of the Potomac River on the Harpers Ferry side was the location of a majority of the buildings of the US Armory. Lower Town is at the point of the confluence of the river, while the Camp Hill section of town can be seen on the hillside. (Courtesy of Library of Congress.)

By the 1920s, when this photograph was taken, Harpers Ferry was again prospering. This photograph shows hotels, a restaurant, a barbershop, a drugstore, and other businesses along Shenandoah Street. The Hotel Conner, the first building on the left, stood where John Brown's Fort is now situated in the park. The hotel advertised rooms for $2 per day in 1903 with steam heat, artesian water, and electric lights. (Courtesy of Library of Congress.)

Another important part of the park today is the buildings of Storer College. Storer College was chartered by the State of West Virginia in 1867 and would constitute an institution of learning for African Americans until its closure in 1955. Depicted here are some of the buildings of Storer College, which sat at the top of the hill above Lower Town. (Courtesy of National Park Service.)

While the town tried repeatedly to rebuild in the late 1800s and early 1900s, each time the efforts were thwarted by devastating floods. As depicted in this 1924 photograph, the Potomac River crested 27.4 feet above normal levels. *National Geographic* described Harpers Ferry in 1945 after a "succession of floods" as looking "like an Italian hill village after the Nazis left, bereft of individuals and trade alike." (Courtesy of Library of Congress.)

There have been at least 46 major floods in Harpers Ferry since 1747. The floods of 1924, 1936, and 1942 would be the final death knell for businesses. The remnants of the cotton mill on Virginius Island are depicted here after the 1924 flood. This same building can be seen in the 1857 lithograph appearing on page 14 (four-story building depicted at far left). (Courtesy of Library of Congress.)

This photograph captures the devastation wrought by the March 1936 flood, which had the highest level of floodwaters in the town's history, with the Potomac River cresting at 36.5 feet above average levels. Ironically, but for the repeated destructive floods that prevented industries and commerce from flourishing, there would be no national park today. The floods paradoxically preserved many features in the present-day park. (Courtesy of Library of Congress.)

A few days after the 1936 floodwaters receded, Congressman Jennings Randolph visited Harpers Ferry and surveyed the damage. He later commented, "If you should ask me when the project that culminated in the Harpers Ferry National Monument was born I would answer you by saying that it was on that day in March 1936 in the mud of the rivers down below." (Courtesy of Jefferson County Museum.)

Two

CREATION OF THE PARK

As longtime resident Raymond Biller attested in an oral history interview, "way before the park came, there were tourists coming to town. Not like they come now but they were here. They'd mostly come by car, but sometimes there were excursion trains." This 1920 photograph, titled "Harpers Ferry Tour" by the Library of Congress, depicts just such tourists driving through Harpers Ferry. (Courtesy of Library of Congress.)

There were many structures and landmarks to see before the establishment of the park. The same group of people pictured on the previous page driving through Harpers Ferry is depicted here atop Jefferson's Rock. Years later, a local recollected that, as a teenager, he would "offer a tour to the people who'd come to see Jefferson Rock and old John Brown's fort." (Courtesy of Library of Congress.)

Then-mayor Gilbert Perry estimated that in the 1890s–1910s, "on weekends and holidays, as many as 28 excursion trains a day brought [people] . . . up from the city" and "society people came from the city for a whole summer, or for a week or two." As seen here, visitors could see tablets discussing Civil War history and an obelisk marking the original location of John Brown's Fort. (Courtesy of National Park Service.)

In addition to tourists, many organizations held meetings in town. Pictured here is a handful of the 150 men and women who met at Harpers Ferry for four days in 1906 at Storer College for the Niagara Movement. The Niagara Movement called for the improvement of civil rights in the United States. The group was led by W.E.B. Du Bois (fifth from right in the first row). (Courtesy of National Park Service.)

Pictured here in 1896, the DC Colored Women's League made a pilgrimage to John Brown's Fort. The fort had been moved to Murphy's Farm from Chicago, where it had been on display in the 1893 World's Fair. Today, park visitors can visit all four of the locations where John Brown's Fort has been situated in Harpers Ferry since its original erection in 1847. (Courtesy of National Park Service.)

The earliest book on Harpers Ferry, *The Strange Story of Harpers Ferry*, was published by resident Joseph Barry in 1903. Barry wrote an earlier pamphlet-sized book, called *The Annals of Harpers Ferry*, in 1869 and another edition in 1872. This early recording of history by Barry would be indispensable to later park historians and scholars. Depicted here is a man reading Barry's book in 1906. (Courtesy of Library of Congress.)

The man in this 1910 photograph can rightly be called the "father of the Harpers Ferry National Historical Park." Henry T. McDonald arrived in Harpers Ferry in 1899 to assume the office of principal of Storer College, taking over as the second principal from Rev. Nathan Brackett. McDonald is pictured here in front of his school's main building, then called Anthony Memorial Hall. (Courtesy of National Park Service.)

McDonald loved studying the history of the area, and he was also an avid promoter of its natural beauty. Pictured here in 1916 is McDonald (fourth from left in the first row of seated men) with a group of his students and teachers atop Loudoun Heights. The town of Harpers Ferry can be seen behind the group and to the left. (Courtesy of National Park Service.)

McDonald was a charter member of the Jefferson County Historical Society, corresponded with noted Civil War and John Brown scholars, and collected John Brown artifacts for the school. In the 1920s, he assisted with a project of identifying historic landmarks and structures and erecting educational markers at those locations. He is standing at the left of this undated photograph holding a hat and stick. (Courtesy of National Park Service.)

When Congressman Randolph visited after the flood of March 1936, he and the principal walked in the mud around town. Randolph recalled McDonald saying, "We ought to have a national park here," and while "the mud was up to his ankle tops . . . he was looking at the stars." Randolph stated the national park was born that day. This is a family portrait of McDonald. (Author's collection.)

Congressman Jennings Randolph, who later went on to become a senator, should be considered a cofounder of the park. He worked tirelessly meeting with state and federal officials and community groups to ensure support for a park. Randolph introduced two bills in Congress before his third proposed bill was approved in 1944. Senator Randolph is seen here kneeling down and talking to a young boy visiting Harpers Ferry from Iran. (Courtesy of National Park Service.)

Pres. Franklin D. Roosevelt is pictured speaking at the dedication of Great Smoky Mountains National Park on September 2, 1940. On June 30, 1944, President Roosevelt signed legislation creating the Harpers Ferry National Monument; this was done only after Secretary of the Interior Harold Ickes stated that his department would not even request funds to administer the site "during the present war." The bill creating the monument praised Congressman Randolph in being "very diligent in endeavoring to have established this national monument." The legislation went on to say the following: "Committee was impressed with the importance of the project, of its great historic interest, and of the wishes of the local community and the Representative from West Virginia, Mr. Randolph, and felt that this was a case in which Congress itself should fix the boundaries and with certain limitations and the right to accept gifts." (Courtesy of National Park Service; Smoky Mountain Collection.)

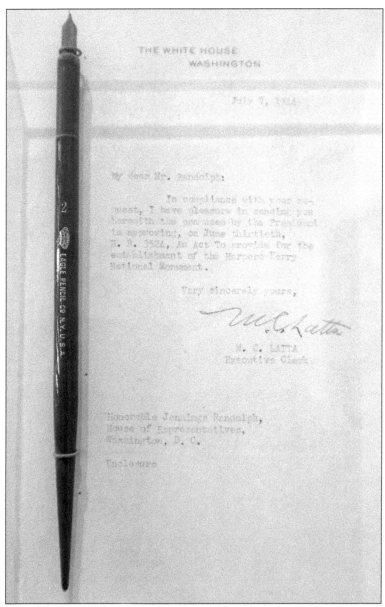

With this pen, President Roosevelt signed legislation creating the Harpers Ferry National Monument. The pen and correspondence, originally sent to Congressman Jennings Randolph, are permanently on display at the Master Armorer House on Shenandoah Street in the Lower Town portion of the park. As important as this pen and signing were, and as hard as many worked to ensure passage of the legislation and support by the president, a lot of work still needed to be done. The enabling legislation created the national monument but with no allocated funds to purchase property. The legislation did allow the park (at that time) to accept donated land for the national monument up to 1,600 acres. So Principal McDonald, Congressman Randolph, and many others set about lobbying various state officials in West Virginia, Virginia, and Maryland for assistance in securing the needed property that fell in each state. The hope was that each state would appropriate funds to buy properties and then turn those properties over to the National Park Service. (Author's collection.)

When the creation of the national monument was announced, some people were very happy. In this photograph from the 1940s, three men appear amused about whatever news is being read. The Library of Congress title for this photograph is "Young Man, Wearing Straw Hat, Reading to Two Men [in] Harpers Ferry." (Courtesy of Library of Congress; photograph by Theodor Jung.)

There was also opposition to the park among local families who might be displaced by the National Park Service. While the 1944 law allowed for the donation of land, no lands or funds were allocated by the legislation. This meant that the boundaries were dependent on state governments securing land through buyouts or eminent domain. These men do not appear to be as pleased as those in the previous photograph. (Courtesy of National Park Service.)

The national monument, and the national park after it, would be charged with preserving and protecting not only historic structures but nature within the park as well. This photograph from the 1950s shows a man next to a very old Virginius Island sycamore tree, which looks to date back to the 1800s. Virginius Island affords present-day visitors a wonderful nature walk and trail. (Courtesy of National Park Service.)

By 1953, West Virginia was able to successfully buy out residents who were still living in Lower Town. In July 1953, several hundred people attended a ceremony at the Harpers Ferry Camp Hill Methodist Church (at left). The ceremony entailed the transfer of a deed for 515 acres from West Virginia to the park. Note the band across the street in this early-1950s photograph. (Courtesy of National Park Service.)

A March 1957 *National Geographic* journalist and visitor to the national monument commented the following: "I felt as if I had come upon a ghost town. Buildings stood deserted, deteriorating. Gray walls of heavy fieldstone gaped with empty window openings. Through them I glimpsed fallen rafters, creeping vegetation, and tattered bits of open sky. It seemed ages, not just years, since people could have lived here and worked here." It would take a lot of hard work during the 1950s to make the national monument presentable. As the monument's first park ranger, John Willett, commented, few individuals "were surprised to learn Harpers Ferry would not be transferred into a fully developed park overnight." Making the park operational would mean conducting historical studies and making many decisions on countless structures that fell within the boundaries of the park. Some of these decisions were hard and involved whether to demolish or restore certain buildings, depending on the age of the structure or if the structure had some unique architectural merit. Chapter Five, starting at page 79, covers those tough decisions. (Courtesy of National Park Service.)

In this early-1950s photograph, early visitors are seen walking around Shenandoah Street before any major work appears to have been initiated. While each building needed restoration work, the buildings on the right side of the road needed far more work than those depicted on the left side. (Courtesy of National Park Service.)

The oldest building in the park is the Harper House. The town founder, Robert Harper, began constructing his home in the 1750s, but it would not be completed until 1782. Thomas Jefferson likely stayed in the house in 1783, and George Washington stayed in the house in 1785. The house was in very poor condition, as pictured in this 1953 photograph. (Courtesy of National Park Service.)

Adjacent to the Harper House is a block of three buildings known as Marmion Row, built in the early 1800s by Robert Harper's descendants. Depicted here is the Wager House, the building next to the Harper House on Marmion Row. This 1956 photograph shows a tree growing up through the roof of the house. (Courtesy of National Park Service.)

Perhaps no photograph illustrates the amount of work needed to be done on the historic structures better than this one from 1956. This photograph shows the front side of Marmion Row and the Wager House, the oldest set of houses in the park. Note the poor condition of the roof and the severe damage to the top floor especially. (Courtesy of National Park Service.)

This 1956 photograph shows the condition of the inside of the Wager House. This is the view out of the gaping holes on the top floor of the Wager House, depicted in the previous photograph. The mountain to the right is Loudoun Heights, and part of the confluence of the Shenandoah and Potomac Rivers can be seen out the "window" as well. (Courtesy of National Park Service.)

Despite the fact that restoration was just beginning, visitors flocked to the monument. It was estimated that 61,000 visited the monument in 1955 and over 100,000 the following year. Visitors traveling by automobile would usually reach the monument by Route 340. This 1963 photograph shows the sign that was posted on Route 340 right at its intersection with Shenandoah Street. (Courtesy of National Park Service.)

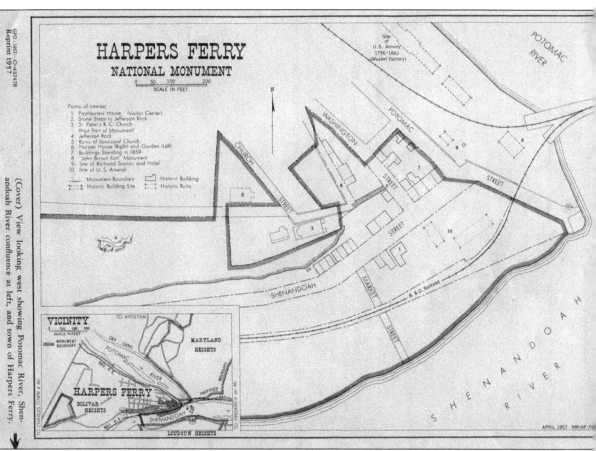

In March 1951, West Virginia appropriated $350,000 for the acquisition of 515 acres of land in Lower Town, as well as portions of Loudoun Heights and Bolivar Heights. Bolivar Heights is about one mile west of Lower Town. In 1953, West Virginia transferred the deeds to the National Park Service. This 1957 map of the Harpers Ferry National Monument shows both the boundaries and points of interest for visitors. An additional 30 acres of land from the old Storer College campus on Camp Hill were donated to the park in 1960, three years after this map was printed. Approximately 20 college buildings came with this transfer of land. Four of the buildings that were part of Storer College were original armory residences for the top-ranking armory officials. Then, three years after the acquisition of the Storer College campus, Maryland donated a total of 763 acres of land on Maryland Heights. Thus, this map was accurate from its printing date of 1957 until 1960, when another map needed to be created. (Author's collection.)

This 1955 photograph was taken atop Maryland Heights, Maryland, and shows the national monument boundaries in Lower Town (bottom center), Camp Hill (the plateau at the top of the hill above Lower Town and starting at the town cemetery visible in this photograph), and Bolivar Heights (top center). To the bottom right of this photograph, the three rectangular boxes represent the original foundations of three armory buildings. At the bottom left, there is a single building. Above that building and directly across the railroad tracks is a cluster of additional buildings. Those buildings, as well as the building at the bottom left, would all be demolished as the park began its renovations in Lower Town. The cluster of buildings all sat atop the buried ruins of the foundations of the US Arsenal (previously depicted on page 13). This photograph can also be compared with the photograph that appears on pages 20 and 21 to see how the town (now park) had changed in the previous 50 years. (Courtesy of National Park Service.)

Visitors could plan out their day and sites to see by reference wall maps, like the one pictured here. This particular display dates to after 1968, as John Brown's Fort (see No. 19 on the map) is shown in Lower Town. From 1896 to 1909, John Brown's Fort was at Murphy's Farm, and it was located on the Storer College campus from 1909 to 1968. (Courtesy of Jefferson County Museum.)

This 1920 photograph shows Maryland Heights from the Harpers Ferry train depot on the opposite side of the Potomac River. Acquiring the front slope and peak of Maryland Heights was extremely important for the development of the park. Henry McDonald partnered with Mary Mish, a powerful and energetic promoter of historical preservation. (Courtesy of National Park Service.)

Mary Mish can be seen here speaking to a crowd of approximately 10,000 people on the fourth day of the John Brown Centennial in October 1959. Mish was instrumental in ensuring that Maryland Heights would be included in the park. At this event, in a ceremony, the park was given a "token presentation" of over 600 acres by Maryland. (Courtesy of National Park Service.)

In this photograph from the 1950s, Gilbert Perry poses atop Jefferson's Rock. Perry served as mayor of Harpers Ferry from 1949 to 1957 and 1963 to 1965. When McDonald died in 1951, Mish continued working with Mayor Perry to ensure Maryland Heights would be included in the park. (Courtesy of National Park Service.)

This 1958 photograph next to John Brown's Fort shows, from left to right, (first row) Bradley Nash, Conrad Wirth, and Gilbert Perry; (second row) unidentified and Frank Anderson. Conrad Wirth was director of the National Park Service from 1951 to 1964 and was a well-known American conservationist, and Frank Anderson was the second Harpers Ferry park superintendent (1958–1962). (Courtesy of National Park Service.)

This 1965 photograph depicts two giants in the history of Harpers Ferry, Sen. Jennings Randolph (left) and Bradley Nash (right). Nash's governmental career spanned multiple presidential administrations from Herbert Hoover to Dwight Eisenhower. He also served as deputy assistant secretary of the Air Force and deputy undersecretary of commerce under Eisenhower and as mayor of Harpers Ferry (1971–1977 and 1983–1987). Nash was intricately involved in promoting the park and donated his land to the park. (Courtesy of National Park Service.)

The Harpers Ferry National Monument was wildly successful, and hundreds of thousands of individuals visited in its first eight years of existence. According to the then newly elected US senator Jennings Randolph, the term "monument" was never appropriate, as it did "not convey the vast scope of history and natural grandeur which are to be found at Harpers Ferry." Because of the national monument's popularity, Pres. John F. Kennedy approved legislation elevating the Harpers Ferry National Monument to one of America's newest national historical parks. President Kennedy had a keen interest in Civil War history and had visited the Gettysburg battlefield on March 31, 1963, and Antietam on April 7, 1963. Brother attorney general Robert Kennedy hiked 50 miles on the Chesapeake & Ohio Canal, ending at Harpers Ferry, in February 1963. President Kennedy signed this legislation on May 29, 1963. This pen and correspondence, originally sent to Sen. Jennings Randolph, are permanently on display at the Master Armorer House in Lower Town. (Author's collection.)

Three

STABILIZATION
AND RESTORATION

This 1953 photograph shows how Shenandoah Street looked when the various properties were first acquired by West Virginia from private landowners and then transferred to the National Park Service and before any restoration or stabilization work could be started. Note the telephone poles and wires. These would be removed and buried under street level by the 1960s. (Courtesy of Library of Congress.)

Some buildings required much more work than others. This 1956 photograph shows clearly the amount of work that must be done on this historic building. Note the surveying instrument in front. This building, called the McCabe-Marmion Building, was built in 1845. After extensive renovation, the building now contains the Industrial Museum, where visitors may learn about early industry in the town. (Courtesy of Library of Congress.)

Fortunately, a few of the buildings were decently preserved and required less preservation efforts upon transfer to the National Park Service than others. This substantial brick residence was built in 1858–1859 for the master armorer. Because of its sound condition, the building was immediately designated as the visitors' center for the national monument. (Courtesy of National Park Service.)

Before work could even be done on the structures, the insides of the properties had to be cleaned out. This 1957 photograph shows an inside hallway in one of the oldest properties. The surveying historian noted the following: "Ceiling boards rotted, mold-covered, wet. Stockpile of Flat Stone in right corner, three timbers on floor said to be from Reel Boats. Stair in wall beyond door completely rotted." (Courtesy of National Park Service.)

This 1956 photograph illustrates that it was not just rotted building material and debris that needed to be removed from the properties. Some departing residents left behind belongings. This photograph shows a room in the historic Wager House where miscellaneous bottles and items were left in a corner cabinet. (Courtesy of National Park Service.)

Two men are moving items out of a building on Shenandoah Street in the mid-1950s. One man (left) appears to be holding curtains or bedding, while the other man (right) is holding a window pane. Note the men are moving the items into a flatbed truck that already looks largely full. Note also the table between the two men. (Courtesy of National Park Service.)

In addition to doing extensive historical surveys on each building, park architects had to assess the amount of work that needed to be completed. Here, two park officials are looking at a decayed roofline to determine if the roof needs to be entirely removed and replaced. Note the plant (bottom left) growing on the third floor of this house. (Courtesy of National Park Service.)

Upon occasion, park employees would find remnants like tools or weapons from the pre–Civil War armory days left by soldiers quartered in the homes. Pictured here in December 1955 are two unidentified park employees; the man on the right is pointing out where a Civil War minié ball was found lodged in a beam. Not only was virtually every home hit by cannon or rifle fire during the war, the houses were all occupied by soldiers. In a letter to a Harpers Ferry resident who had fled, the writer stated, "I tell you, Mary, the Ferry looks awful. You know I was attached to it as much as anyone but I can truly say I don't want to go back there to live until it is built up again. The soldiers that are there are all strangers. The houses look awful, the windows are all broken. Your house is all shot up, the soldiers had been in it but there is none there now. There was a great many pictures drawn on the wall that the soldiers had been drawing." (Courtesy of National Park Service.)

This graffiti was found when park employees were restoring the Susan Downey House on High Street. The house was built in 1838–1839. Today, the building houses an exhibit on the Battle of Harpers Ferry. Pvt. W.H. Shuster's unit, the Philadelphia Fire Zouaves, was garrisoned in Harpers Ferry approximately one week after the Battles of Harpers Ferry and Antietam. It is likely he left his graffiti at that time. After the surrender of 12,400 Union soldiers to the Confederate army, the Union soldiers were marched out of town and could not take up arms again until paroled. The Confederate forces quickly left Harpers Ferry to join in the battle occurring at Antietam on September 17, 1862. When the Confederate forces retreated south after Antietam, Gen. George B. McClellan had a great majority of his 80,000-man Army of the Potomac stationed in and around Harpers Ferry. Every house was used as quarters or shelter during this time period. One wonders whether Pvt. W.H. Shuster got to see President Lincoln when the president visited Harpers Ferry on October 1–2, 1862. (Author's collection.)

Not only the interior of buildings had to be inspected but also the exteriors. Pictured here is the first superintendent of the Harpers National Monument, Edwin Dale (second from left), who served in Harpers Ferry from 1955 to 1957. The group is inspecting the exterior of the Philip Coons Building, which was built in 1845–1846. (Courtesy of National Park Service.)

This photograph shows the Philip Coons Building in 1956 as restoration was just beginning. The two men on ladders appear to be repointing and strengthening the mortar between the stonework on the front of the building. Note that the balcony above the heads of the men lacks a floor. (Courtesy of National Park Service.)

When Coons constructed this building in 1845, the first floor was designed for commercial stores, with residential rooms on the second floor. However, Coons was a member of the Harpers Ferry Masonic Lodge (Charity Lodge No. 111) and agreed to allow the Masons to develop the third floor as a lodge for their meetings. (Courtesy of Library of Congress.)

While not open to the general public, the third floor of the Philip Coons Building has an elliptical vaulted ceiling unique among the surviving buildings of the park. Additionally, the beams of the vaulted ceiling were constructed from salvaged wood from the famous "gundalow" boats that navigated the Shenandoah River in the late 1700s and early 1800s. (Courtesy of Library of Congress.)

To the right of the Philip Coons Building, a group of eight men works to stabilize and restore the exterior of the McCabe-Marmion Building. This three-story building was originally constructed in 1845. Work on the interior of this building would not be restoration. Rather, the interior was entirely rebuilt in the late 1950s, as illustrated in the next several photographs. (Courtesy of National Park Service.)

This photograph was taken standing inside the McCabe-Marmion Building in 1956 and shows the skeleton of the second and third stories of the building. The adjacent building, which can be seen in the top center of the photograph, is the Kaplan Department Store Building. As will be discussed in Chapter Five, the Kaplan Building was entirely demolished in 1961. (Courtesy of National Park Service.)

This 1961 photograph was taken from inside the building looking out toward Shenandoah Street. Out the openings on the right, one can see the raised railroad tracks of the Winchester & Potomac line. Looking out the center two doors, one can see the James McGraw Building, which as of 2020 houses the Harpers Ferry: A Place in Time exhibit. (Courtesy of National Park Service.)

Men are seen up on scaffolding working on rebuilding the backside of the McCabe-Marmion Building. Across the street, two men with a wheelbarrow can also be seen working on the James McGraw Building. The empty space to the left of the McCabe-Marmion Building was previously occupied by the four-story Kaplan Department Store Building. It was razed earlier in the year. (Courtesy of National Park Service.)

Pictured here are the Philip Coons Building and the McCabe-Marmion Building after restoration and rebuilding were completed. Restroom facilities for the park are currently located in the bottom floor of the Philip Coons Building, and the McCabe-Marmion Building houses exhibits on industry in Harpers Ferry and on the history of Virginius Island. (Courtesy of Library of Congress.)

To the left of the Philip Coons and McCabe-Marmion Buildings sits the 2.5-story John G. Wilson Building, originally built in 1825–1826 and then expanded in 1834. Occasionally, local residents referred to the building as the old Stagecoach Inn, as stagecoaches reputedly dropped passengers off in front of this building. The building is pictured here before renovations. (Courtesy of National Park Service.)

Pictured here is the John G. Wilson Building in 1962, prior to the beginning of renovations. Note the sign in the window on the first floor. The sign refers to the building as the "Stagecoach Inn, built in 1834 [and] being restored as a new visitor center." (Courtesy of National Park Service.)

From 1956 to 1966, a visitor would encounter numerous signs like this one either adjacent or affixed to buildings being built or restored. The sign pictured here was adjacent to the renovations then occurring at the Harper House. National Park Service director Conrad Wirth proposed a 10-year campaign (called "Mission 66") to modernize the infrastructure and resources of the national parks by 1966. (Courtesy of National Park Service.)

Pictured here in 1965 is the Stagecoach Inn after it opened as the park's then-new visitors' center. Today, the building houses the Park Bookshop and the Harpers Ferry Park Association. Founded in 1971, the Harpers Ferry Park Association is a nonprofit organization dedicated to supporting the park's educational mission. The park association has also generated millions of dollars in support of the park. (Courtesy of National Park Service.)

This 1956 photograph shows three structures on the left-hand side of the very beginning of Potomac Street in Lower Town. The first building (left) and the third building (right) were determined by the National Park Service to be historically significant to the 1859–1865 time period, while the building in the center was not. In the first step of renovating these structures, the middle building would be removed. (Courtesy of National Park Service.)

This 1957 photograph shows two of the three structures depicted in the previous photograph. White Hall Tavern (left) was originally built in 1838–1839 and made into a tavern in 1847. Frederick Roeder's confectionary store (right) was erected in 1856. Note above White Hall Tavern that restoration work can be seen on the front side of the Wager House on Marmion Row. (Courtesy of National Park Service.)

Frederick Roeder's confectionary store is depicted in this 1957 photograph. The house has been stabilized, and the restoration process has just commenced. All of the buildings behind Roeder's store are also being restored. A "Mission 66" sign can be seen to the left of Roeder's store. (Courtesy of National Park Service.)

This 1950s photograph depicts the backside of White Hall Tavern. This tavern began operating around 1847 and was probably operated from 1847 until 1861. The front side of this building sits on Potomac Street. Before the Civil War, the armory complex sat on the other side of Potomac Street. As such, park historians have estimated that armory workers likely walked across Potomac Street to imbibe at this establishment in the late 1840s and 1850s. The backside of this structure presented a unique architecture detail. Each of the buildings that the National Park Service restored underwent extensive historical research. This unique architectural feature did indeed open up into the inside of the back of the tavern. Was this an outhouse that actually connected to the back of the tavern so that clientele did not have to go out into the cold weather in search of a privy? Did other Civil War–era homes have such extensions? These are the type of mysterious questions that early park employees were faced with when researching and restoring these structures. (Courtesy of National Park Service.)

This photograph, taken from the back porch of Frederick Roeder's house, shows the backside of Frederick Roeder's store (left) and White Hall Tavern (right). In this photograph, early park restoration strategies are revealed. The backside of the White Hall Tavern now shows a door where the unique architectural detail previously existed. Frederick Roeder was a patriotic German immigrant living in Harpers Ferry. Roeder ran a confectionery and very likely provide various treats to the local armory workers. When the Civil War started, Frederick Roeder decided to stay in Harpers Ferry when a majority of the population of the town fled. Part of the Confederate army occupied Harpers Ferry from late April 1861 to June 1861. When the Confederates left town, Roeder mused, "We have got rid of that lot and have escaped at least with our lives; but what will the next party that comes do to us?" On July 4, 1861, the staunch Unionist Roeder went down to water's edge and was struck and killed by an errant shot fired by a Union soldier. (Courtesy of Library of Congress.)

The view depicted here shows the intersection of Potomac Street and Hog Alley. At the top of Hog Alley is Frederick Roeder's house. At the corner of the two streets is Frederick Roeder's store. To the left of Frederick Roeder's store is the White Hall Tavern. All the buildings have been restored by the time of this photograph. (Courtesy of Library of Congress.)

This 1957 photograph depicts the restoration and renovations on the front side of the Wager House on Marmion Row. The reader can compare the renovations to the original condition of this building shown on the bottom of page 37. This row of structures is the oldest set of residences that still survives in the park. (Courtesy of National Park Service.)

This 1958 photograph depicts the backside of the Wager House on Marmion Row. Here, men are replacing the entire roof. To the right of the Wager House is the Harper House, the oldest surviving structure in the park. Construction on the Harper House was completed in 1782. The Wager House (for Robert Harper's descendants) was slowly constructed from 1800 to 1833. (Courtesy of National Park Service.)

Renovations to the Wager House moved swiftly. By the end of 1958, and at the time this photograph was taken, the roof on the Wager House was completely rebuilt (although the underside was not yet finished) and a front porch was added to the Wager House as well. Renovations were occurring in the next section of Marmion Row (right). (Courtesy of National Park Service.)

This 1964 photograph shows the completed renovations and restorations on the Wager House and Marmion Row. The road to the center of this photograph is Hog Alley, which intersects High Street at the top of hill (behind the truck) and Potomac Street at the bottom. Renovations to Frederick Roeder's house (left of the truck) were just commencing. On page 61, the house is shown completed. (Courtesy of National Park Service.)

The first building depicted on the right in this 1950s photograph is the Gerald Bond Wager Building. While the present structure was built in 1837–1838, it is believed that the log cabin of the town's first settler (Peter Stephens) was on this location. (Courtesy of National Park Service.)

This photograph of the Gerald Bond Wager House (and the three adjoining houses) was taken in 1955, just prior to restorations to this structure. The only notable change made by the National Park Service at this time was a plaque placed on the side of the building. (Courtesy of National Park Service.)

By the late 1950s, major renovations were undertaken at the Gerald Bond Wager House. Note the split-rail fencing meant to keep people away from the building while renovations were underway. (Courtesy of National Park Service.)

This 1961 photograph shows that all the renovations (for now) to the buildings in this section of Shenandoah Street were completed. The Gerald Bond Wager Building would house exhibits on John Brown. This building continues to be used to interpret John Brown's story. Note how the three buildings adjacent to the Gerald Bond Wager Building all use their windows to display exhibits and artifacts. (Courtesy of National Park Service.)

Sometimes renovating and rebuilding are never really completed. This 1976 photograph shows the Unseld Building being completely gutted and rebuilt. The Unseld Building is to the left of the Gerald Bond Wager Building. (Courtesy of National Park Service.)

This early-1950s photograph shows the state of disrepair of the Harper House. The house would not be completely restored and open to the public until 1963. For the first 20 years of the park's existence in Harpers Ferry, visitors could examine the exterior of the building but not the inside. (Courtesy of National Park Service.)

By 1972, the Harper House and grounds were completely restored. Additionally, the wooden walkway connecting the Harper House to the Harper House Gardens was rebuilt to match the same walkway shown in a late-1800s photograph. Today, the bridge over to the garden no longer exists. However, visitors can walk up to the second-floor balcony of the Harper House and look into the rooms on the first and second floors. (Courtesy of National Park Service.)

Four

STONE STEPS TO LOCKWOOD HOUSE

From the earliest days of the park, one of the most popular walks to take started at the corner of Shenandoah and High Streets and up the historic stone steps to the heights beyond. Fabulous views and important landmarks can be seen along this trail. This chapter recreates that walk. Visitors can be seen starting this climb in this 1957 photograph. (Courtesy of National Park Service.)

Before the park, the historic stone steps served as a thoroughfare for townspeople since the early 1800s. The trail connected the upper part of town and Camp Hill to Lower Town. This early-1950s photograph shows the state of the historic stairs at its base. The wooden structure (right) would be quickly removed by the park. To the left of the stairs is a sign that reads "Stone Steps Tavern." Local residents recalled that a tavern, bar, or beer joint occupied this building for much of the early 1900s. The building is now known as the John T. Rieley Building. This is one of the oldest structures in the park, and its construction dates to the period of 1804–1813. Today, the building houses the Black Voices Museum. (Courtesy of National Park Service.)

This 1955 photograph gives the viewer an idea of the condition of the upper part of the trail as one climbed the stone steps from Lower Town. The wooden building in the foreground would be removed in the early days of the park. In the first stage of renovations to buildings in Lower Town, the park "obliterated" numerous wooden shacks and wooden buildings of no apparent historical value. During this time period, the National Park Service used the term "obliterate" or "obliteration" to refer to the demolition of structures that were deemed unsafe or not of historical significance to the park's stated themes. At the top left of this photograph, Maryland Heights can be seen from across the Potomac River. To the bottom right, the patio in front of St. Peter's Catholic Church can be seen. (Courtesy of National Park Service.)

If one was visiting Harpers Ferry National Monument in the late 1950s, the point of departure for the walk up to the Lockwood House would be at the corner of Shenandoah and High Streets. At each point along the way, the National Park Service placed signs to guide the visitor, like the one pictured here in the grassy lot at the corner of the two streets. (Courtesy of National Park Service.)

This late-1950s photograph shows the start of the climb. The steps were carved out of solid rock in the early 1800s. These stairs were labeled the "blood stairs" during the Civil War. Some claim the name was derived from bleeding soldiers who were carried up these stairs for treatment at a hospital at the top of the hill, while others claimed the term came from blood left by horses. (Courtesy of National Park Service.)

Taken in October 1959 during the centennial of the John Brown raid, this photograph depicts the view looking back down the stone steps. Thousands upon thousands of individuals walked up and down these stairs during the four-day John Brown Centennial. (Courtesy of National Park Service.)

Here, a man is looking down the stone steps in the 1950s. The stone steps have been the subject of musings of poets and artists. An 1880s poem reads as follows: "The Stone Steps, anciently carved in virgin rock, A sweet worn town with old world air, A street that climbs on a stone laden stair, To fableland and green plateau, With the Shenandoah's song below." (Courtesy of National Park Service.)

The next building one would encounter climbing up the stone steps is the Harper House, shown here in the late 1950s. Since Robert Harper died a year before it was finished, it was immediately used as a tavern when the construction was finished. Thomas Jefferson likely stayed in the house in 1783, and George Washington lodged there in 1785. (Courtesy of Library of Congress.)

Because they were being professionally studied and surveyed during the 1950s, many of the buildings in the park were not open to visitors, as is indicated by this 1950s sign affixed to the Harper House. The idea was that, with multiple signs like this one, visitors could at least see the exterior of the buildings while the interiors were researched and restored. (Courtesy of National Park Service.)

This 1961 photograph by Jack Boucher shows the walkway down Marmion Row. At this point in the restoration process, the Harper House was very close to opening to the public. The walkway above Marmion Row was constructed at the time of this photograph. Photographs from the 1950s show no bridge connecting the house to the gardens. (Courtesy of National Park Service.)

Clyde King took this photograph in September 1965. It depicts the completed restoration of the Harper House as well as the walkway from the second-story balcony of the Harper House to the Harper House Gardens. (National Park Service.)

After passing the Harper House and Marmion Row, this 1960 visitor then came upon St. Peter's Catholic Church on the left. Local legend suggests that the church survived damage from artillery shells during the Civil War because its leader, Father Costello, would fly the Union Jack to dissuade either the Northern or Southern army from bombing and thereby perchance to insult the sovereignty of the British government. (Courtesy of National Park Service.)

From the very onset of the park's existence in Harpers Ferry, park ranger–guided tours and talks have been a regular feature of a visitor's experience. Pictured here is an early park ranger interacting with visitors. The ranger and visitors are standing in front of St. Peter's Catholic Church, built around 1833, and looking down on the Lower Town and the confluence of the Shenandoah and Potomac Rivers. (Courtesy of National Park Service.)

A visitor continuing up the trail would then see the ruins of St. John Episcopal Church to the right. In 1845, the present structure was built, and it was substantially rebuilt in 1852. The church was reduced to ruins by the Civil War. In 1882, the church was rebuilt again but did not do well in terms of membership, and the structure was sold in 1895. (Courtesy of Library of Congress.)

Then and now, the park has erected many signs throughout to interpret structures and landmarks. This was especially important at times when the park did not have enormous resources to fund frequent ranger-guided tours. The park later engaged in restoration efforts to this building to stabilize it and remove the graffiti. (Courtesy of National Park Service.)

About a quarter-mile beyond the ruins of St. John's Episcopal, Jefferson's Rock appears to the left of the trail. Two small boys in 1961 are looking at the same view Pres. Thomas Jefferson looked at in October 1783. (Courtesy of National Park Service.)

From Jefferson's Rock and again going up the trail only a few feet, the cemetery is on the right up a short incline of stone steps. In this 1961 photograph, taken by Lee Maynard, one can see a large tree had subsumed Harper's 1782 burial plot, the first grave in the four-acre cemetery. The tree has been removed. (Courtesy of National Park Service.)

Walking to the top of the cemetery, one comes into view of the backside of the 1847 Lockwood House. The first floor was built for the armory paymaster's quarters. A second story was added in 1858. During the Civil War, the house served as the headquarters of Union general Henry Lockwood, thereby earning its name. Philip Sheridan also used this building in 1864. (Courtesy of Library of Congress.)

The Lockwood House would be transferred from the federal government to Storer College in 1869, and the very first classes of Storer College were taught in this building. During Storer College's ownership, a third story was added. When the federal government reacquired the building in 1960, in order to be historically accurate, the third story was removed. (Courtesy of Library of Congress.)

THE WAR IN UPPER VIRGINIA—GEN. SHERIDAN'S HEADQUARTERS AT HARPER'S FERRY.—FROM A SKETCH BY OUR SPECIAL ARTIST, J. E. TAYLOR.

Often asked is how the National Park Service decides how to renovate certain buildings. The park engages experts to study the structure and its history. Images of the structure from the time period to which it is to be restored are especially helpful. Depicted here is an 1864 wood engraving of the Lockwood House. Note the columns and its two stories and compare with the following photograph. (Courtesy of Library of Congress.)

While the exterior of the Lockwood House now appears pristinely restored to visitors, a substantial amount of restoration work needs to be accomplished to the inside. In 2017, the National Park Service and the Harpers Ferry Park Association secured a major grant to renovate the interior of the structure as well. (Courtesy of Library of Congress.)

Five

HARD CHOICES AND STRATEGIC DECISIONS

This 1959 photograph showing the demolition of a Victorian-era structure on Shenandoah Street might surprise some at first glance. Why would the National Park Service be demolishing buildings from the late 1880s? Part of the decision, as will be illustrated in the following pages of this chapter, is that this and other Victorian-era buildings stood atop the remains of the US Arsenal Square. (Courtesy of National Park Service.)

Pictured in the early 1950s is the east end of Shenandoah Street. Maryland Heights can be seen in the distance beyond the end of the street. On the right, three Victorian-era buildings are visible. Behind these are several other buildings from the late 1800s to early 1900s. None of these buildings exist in the park today. (Courtesy of National Park Service.)

This mid-1950s photograph was taken from a spot a little farther to the west on Shenandoah Street but still facing east towards Maryland Heights. The substantial Victorian building pictured just after the automobile on the right-hand side of the road was another building constructed atop Arsenal Square. The three buildings in the previous photograph are beyond this building (and towards Maryland Heights). (Courtesy of National Park Service.)

This photograph was taken in 1959. The park erected the sign in the space behind the row of buildings depicted in the previous two photographs. The sign was erected because otherwise the visitors would not realize they were standing atop the remains of Arsenal Square. When these groups were excavated later, amazing archaeological discoveries were unearthed. (Courtesy of National Park Service.)

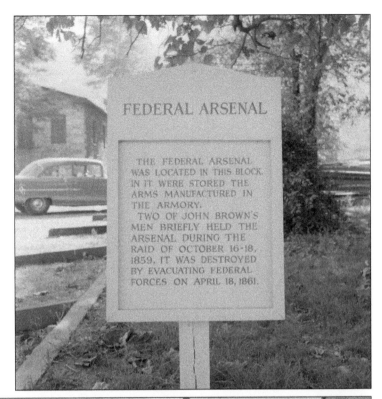

The building in the foreground (left) stood where the Hotel Connor stood in the early 1900s. The building to the right of this building and behind stood on the approximate site of the first major arsenal building constructed in Harpers Ferry (see page 13). These two buildings were also slated for demolition in order to excavate Arsenal Square. (Courtesy of National Park Service.)

This December 1864 drawing by Alfred R. Waud was indispensable in helping park officials create how the left side of Shenandoah Street (looking west) appeared during the Civil War. This Civil War drawing is titled "General Stevensons Headquarters—Harpers Ferry." The soldier in the foreground stands at the intersection of Shenandoah and Potomac Streets. The building on the right is the Gerald Bond Wager Building (see pages 63–65). Historians know that Gen. John Stevenson's headquarters was in the Master Armorer House (center building in this drawing). Loudoun Heights can be seen behind the Master Armorer House. All of the buildings discussed in the last four pages of this chapter did not exist before 1865. As the park has tried to preserve Lower Town as best as possible as it existed between 1859 (the year of John Brown's raid) and 1865, the removal of these buildings adhered with this mission. (Courtesy of Library of Congress.)

This photograph captures another building being demolished on Shenandoah Street. After this building, the final building to be obliterated on this section of Shenandoah Street is the one seen just behind the tree (and to the right of building being demolished in this photograph). Comparing this image to the 1864 Alfred Waud drawing on the previous page, one can see how the demolitions returned this area of the park to its Civil War–era appearance. Some preservationists, both then and now, have lamented the destruction of Victorian-era architecture within the park. From the perspective of the managers of the park over time, two of the early stated reasons for preserving Harpers Ferry as a park was to recollect historic events pertaining to either John Brown's raid or the Civil War. As such, when the park reacquired the central part of Lower Town, virtually all Victorian buildings were removed. One building still exists on Shenandoah Street (the James McGraw Building) and one on High Street (the Burton Watchshop). (Courtesy of National Park Service.)

This 1965 photograph shows Arsenal Square cleared of postbellum buildings. Arsenal Square was where thousands and thousands of finished muskets and rifles were stored. The square consisted of a large arsenal depot, built in 1799–1800; a small arsenal depot, built in 1806–1807; and a one-story superintendent's office, built in 1832. The square foundation in the center of this photograph marks the superintendent's office. (Courtesy of National Park Service.)

In 1959, archaeologists were able to dig up the foundations of all three of the major buildings in Arsenal Square. In fact, archaeologists were able to dig down to the cellar level and find intact stairs, bricked floors, and other details. Workers also found melted muskets, rifles, and other gun parts that were left in the arsenal ruins when the buildings were torched in April 1861. (Courtesy of National Park Service.)

Visitors in October 1959 are looking into the archaeology trenches, which show walls and the foundation of the small arsenal. This two-story brick building was constructed in 1806–1807. When the US Army set fire to this building in April 1861 to avoid it falling into Confederate hands, 15,000 muskets and rifles were destroyed. (Courtesy of National Park Service.)

On a wintry day in 1964, the approximate boundaries of the small arsenal building can still be seen. In the park today, one can walk the contours of where the small arsenal and large arsenal buildings once stood. Interpretative signs, then and now, help tell the story of Arsenal Square. (Courtesy of National Park Service.)

Approaching Lower Town via Shenandoah Street, this 1953 photograph depicts the Catholic School of Harpers Ferry (left-hand side of the road). The Catholic school was built in 1886. When park officials inspected the building, they found an arch stone in the cellar that once stood above the main entrance with the year 1886 inscribed on it. (Courtesy of National Park Service.)

This 1953 photograph depicts the front of the 1886 Catholic school. In the late 1920s and 1930s, the building was converted to a movie theater called the Tri-State Theater. Residents used it during the Great Depression. Locals petitioned the park to preserve the building, but the park determined that the building had "little architectural merit." (Courtesy of National Park Service.)

Buildings constructed after 1859–1865 were slated for demolition in the 1950s as not relating to the park's then-defined themes of the Civil War or John Brown's raid. In addition to the buildings on Arsenal Square, the Catholic school, the Kaplan Building, and the Scottish castle are examples of buildings slated for demolition. Pictured here in 1953 is the demolition of the Catholic school. (Courtesy of National Park Service.)

The biggest building on Shenandoah Street was that of the Kaplan Department Store, owned by Jewish merchant Abe Kaplan, pictured at far right of this photograph. The four-story building was constructed in the 1890s and boasted the only elevator in town. It had a tall front of glazed bricks. When the building was demolished in 1956, a cornerstone was found that contained a Hebrew bible from 1883. (Courtesy of National Park Service.)

This photograph from the early 1950s shows Whitman Avenue leading up to Bolivar Heights. Whitman Avenue was named after Royal Emerson Whitman, who served as a Union officer during the Civil War. Despite being from Maine, he was attracted to the area and purchased land from Storer College to build his home. The ridge line at the top of this road (top center of photograph) is properly referred to as Bolivar Heights. The sweeping fields to the left and right of the road were the approximate location of the surrendering of the 12,400-man Union army garrison in Harpers Ferry. Union regiments stood in formation on these fields and took an oath not to fight again for the North or aid in the war effort until they were properly exchanged, or paroled, for captured Southern soldiers. The parole system, as it was known, would be discontinued in 1863. Note the silhouette of Whitman's Scottish castle on the top left of this photograph. (Courtesy of National Park Service.)

Pictured here in the 1950s is Whitman's Scottish castle. The inside featured murals in each room. Whitman was said to have styled the construction of this building after those found in medieval Scotland. Thus, the building became known to locals as the "Scottish castle." Whitman moved to Washington, DC, in the early 1900s and left the building to new owners. Local resident Raymond Biller said that, in the 1920s–1930s, "at Christmas time, [they] would have parties for us kids—they'd have a school bus haul us up to their Scottish Castle up on Bolivar Heights." The last few years before the park acquired the building and land, the structure was already abandoned. When the park acquired the building, it had already been subjected to vandalism and neglect. The park decided to tear the building down in 1963. (Courtesy of Library of Congress.)

This 1965 photograph was taken just two years after the Scottish castle was torn down. In this photograph, Whitman Avenue is shown just behind the new park sign announcing, "Bolivar Heights Unit." Bolivar Heights was the site of multiple Civil War engagements, including the Battle of Bolivar Heights in October 1861. (Courtesy of National Park Service.)

The visitors in this 1960s photograph are standing approximately where the Scottish castle once sat. In addition to the Battle of Bolivar Heights, this is good location to study the terrain involved in the 1862 Siege of Harpers Ferry by Confederate forces. (Courtesy of National Park Service.)

The park had many hard decisions to make regarding the old Storer College campus as well. Storer College closed in 1955, and the National Park Service acquired the campus and all associated buildings. Some buildings, like Storer College's main administrative building, Anthony Memorial Hall, pictured here, would be used for a new East Coast training center for park rangers, called the Stephen T. Mather Training Center. (Courtesy of Library of Congress.)

While Anthony Memorial Hall would be converted into the Mather Training Center, other campus buildings would become part of Harpers Ferry National Historical Park. These buildings included the Lockwood House, Brackett House, Curtiss Freewill Baptist Church, and Morrell House. The Morrell House, pictured in 1968, houses the park administration. (Courtesy of National Park Service.)

Pictured here is Mosher Hall, a dormitory for students of Storer College. It sat next to Anthony Memorial Hall (the corner of which can be seen on the left margin of the photograph). By the 1960s, the building was outdated and needed many repairs. (Courtesy of National Park Service.)

Pictured here is the obliteration of Mosher Hall. Several other Storer College buildings were demolished as well, including the President's House. However, the Lockwood House, Brackett House, and Morrell House were important to restore, because these buildings were all residences for armory officials before the Civil War. The right wing of Anthony Memorial Hall was the armory superintendent's residence. (Courtesy of Library of Congress.)

Another strategic decision the park faced was what to do with John Brown's Fort. Originally built in 1847, it was relocated to the Chicago World's Fair in 1893, then reconstructed on Murphy's Farm outside of Harpers Ferry in 1896, and then moved to the Storer College campus in 1909. Storer College used the fort as a museum, as seen in this undated photograph. (Courtesy of National Park Service.)

Despite some local opposition, the decision was made to move John Brown's Fort to Lower Town. This decision was made, in part, because the fort occupied space that might impinge on the new National Park Service Interpretive Design Center, which was to be erected in that same general area. This 1968 photograph shows the fort being prepared for its fourth journey. (Courtesy of National Park Service.)

John Brown's Fort is seen here traveling down Shenandoah Street. The whole process of moving the fort from the old Storer College campus to Lower Town and settling the building in Arsenal Square was completed in just one day. (Courtesy of National Park Service.)

This 1972 photograph depicts the current location of John Brown's Fort at the edge of Arsenal Square. At the time of the fort's move in 1968, the original location of the fort in Lower Town was privately owned, so the fort was moved to Arsenal Square. However, in 2001, the park received ownership of the original site, which is approximately 100 yards away—making a fifth move possible. (Courtesy of National Park Service.)

This 1961 photograph, taken from Harpers Ferry, shows Maryland Heights. Above the railroad tunnel and to the left is a 1905 advertisement that was painted on the side of Maryland Heights. This advertisement reads, "Mennen's Borated Talcum Toilet Powder." (Courtesy of National Park Service.)

The park gave permission for a preservation group to try to remove the old painted advertisement from the side of Maryland Heights. This 1963 photograph shows a family of five watching as workers scale down the side of Maryland Heights in the attempt to eradicate the advertisement. (Courtesy of National Park Service.)

In this late-1970s photograph, mountain climbers Ed Bollack (left) and Rob Savoye (right) pose after successfully climbing Maryland Heights. Rob Savoye wrote the first climber's guidebook to Maryland Heights in the 1970s and climbed the face of Maryland Heights many times over the decades. The two are equipped with hooks and ropes and had just finished one of their numerous climbs down the side of Maryland Heights. As of the date of this publication, Maryland Heights has been closed to rock climbers. Despite the 1963 attempt to eradicate the advertisement from the face of Maryland Heights, the Mennen sign is still quite legible in this photograph and to visitors in 2020. To some, the sign is another historical feature in the park and something many visitors view favorably. In the past, the bookstore in Lower Town has even sold postcards and T-shirts showing the Mennen Borated Talcum Toilet Powder sign. (Courtesy of Rob Savoye.)

Six

PARADOXES OF
TRANSPORTATION

The rivers brought early people to Harpers Ferry and powered the waterwheels and turbines that were so essential to early industry. However, the same power of the rivers for industry and transportation could create perils for the town and then park. This September 8, 1996, photograph by David T. Gilbert shows boaters paddling down Shenandoah Street. This flood was caused by rains from Hurricane Fran. (Courtesy of David Gilbert.)

After river travel and travel by horse and carriage and canalboat, the next mode of transportation into Harpers Ferry was by train. The Baltimore & Ohio had reached the shoreline opposite Harpers Ferry by 1834 and had bridged the confluence into town by 1836. From 1836 through the present, trains have continued to take people to the town and now park. This 1959 photograph shows a park ranger waiting for the throngs of people disembarking from special excursion trains to the park for the John Brown Centennial. Loudoun Heights can be seen above the train, and Arsenal Square can be seen in the lower right. It was estimated that the four-day John Brown Centennial in 1959 drew 40,000 people to the park in a four-day period. (Courtesy of National Park Service.)

After the trains came the automobiles. This automobile, even antiquated by 1958 standards when this photograph was taken, is depicted taking a leisurely drive along Shenandoah Street in the early days of the national monument. Note the sign to the right of the car advising, "No Parking This Side." This prohibition was unfortunately soon changed, to the chagrin of many—as the reader will see shortly. (Courtesy of National Park Service.)

In addition to the increased automobile traffic, commercial buses began bringing people to the park as well. Note at least three different full-size commercial buses all unloading or picking up people at the intersection of Shenandoah and Potomac Streets in this October 1959 photograph. Since the 1990s, private commercial buses have been prohibited from Lower Town. (Courtesy of National Park Service.)

By 1963, when this photograph was taken, automobiles and buses careened all over Lower Town. This photograph depicts congestion at the corner of High Street and Shenandoah Street. As car traffic got worse and worse, people began saying that the massive number of automobiles in Lower Town was distracting from the Civil War feel of this area of the park. (Courtesy of National Park Service.)

Automobiles brought people to the park, which was a good thing since the whole idea of a national park is that it should be appreciated and enjoyed by as many Americans as possible. However, the problem soon emerged about where to park all these vehicles. At first, people began parking at the eastern end of Shenandoah Street down by the confluence, as illustrated in this 1956 photograph. (Courtesy of National Park Service.)

By the time this photograph was taken in 1956, the park apparently no longer prohibited or enforced "no parking on this side of road." Now, people were parking on the right side of the road on Shenandoah Street all the way through Lower Town. This photograph was taken from the balcony of the Stagecoach Inn. (Courtesy of National Park Service.)

And on busy days and weekends, park visitors began parking on both sides of Shenandoah Street before getting to the main stretch of historic buildings on the street. This 1956 photograph was also taken from the balcony of the Stagecoach Inn but looking west. Note the park ranger (bottom left), who looks to be investigating an issue. (Courtesy of National Park Service.)

On days when the park had one its many celebratory anniversary events, parking would become even more exacerbated. This photograph was taken in October 1959 during the four-day event commemorating the centennial of John Brown's raid. (Courtesy of National Park Service.)

This photograph, also taken during the John Brown Centennial commemorations in October 1959, shows automobiles parked on the left side of Shenandoah Street almost back to the intersection of Route 340, with automobiles on the right inching forwards. Because the park would have many more similar events in the future, park officials began diligently working towards both short-term and long-term solutions. (Courtesy of National Park Service.)

One short-term solution to the problem in Harpers Ferry was to create designated parking lots along the side of the Winchester & Potomac Railroad line. On especially busy days, automobiles would not only be parked between Shenandoah Street and the Winchester line but also in overflow spaces on the other side of the tracks, between the tracks and the Shenandoah River. (Courtesy of National Park Service.)

Another solution implemented by the park is shown in this 1965 photograph. Park rangers were employed as traffic officers and spent time directing traffic and parking. Note the ranger in this photograph is using both hands to direct drivers and traffic in different directions and also appears to be employing a traffic whistle. (Courtesy of National Park Service.)

The long-term solution for the park was the development of a new visitors' center in the early 1990s that was located approximately two miles from Lower Town. This new visitors' center would shuttle visitors down to Lower Town and back by a fleet of park buses. At the podium for the ribbon-cutting ceremony are US senator Robert Byrd (left) and Bradley Nash (right). (Courtesy of National Park Service.)

Senator Byrd (right) and park superintendent Don Campbell (left) are seen here taking the inaugural shuttle bus ride to Lower Town. Senator Byrd, like Sen. Jennings Randolph before him, was a tireless advocate for the park. Don Campbell was the longest-serving park superintendent (1979–2008) and ushered in many improvements to the park during his tenure and was well respected. (Courtesy of National Park Service.)

The rivers brought people to Harpers Ferry and helped people transport goods to market. The rivers were America's first superhighway. Yet the floods constantly threatened Harpers Ferry. The 1924 and 1936 floods ironically set the stage for the establishment of the park. This 1950s photograph shows visitors looking at a flood marker showing the highest three floods, 1936, 1889, and 1942. (Courtesy of National Park Service.)

This family marvels at the flood levels in this 1962 photograph. The markers were moved to this structure when the building in the previous photograph was demolished. The park would not be done with flooding in Harpers Ferry. The park would see major floods in 1972 (the fifth highest flood in Harpers Ferry history), 1985 (the sixth highest), and two in 1996 (including the seventh highest). (Courtesy of National Park Service.)

This 1972 photograph shows that someone taped a paper sign showing how high the 1972 flood got compared to previous floods (just below the top four floods in history). Hurricane Agnes dumped torrents of rain on the area, and the rivers crested at 29.7 feet above normal levels. (Courtesy of National Park Service.)

This 1972 flood photograph shows how far the waters came inwards. This photograph was taken at the intersection of Hog Alley (to the immediate right) and Potomac Street. The photographer is standing in the middle of Potomac Street and looking down the street towards John Brown's Fort. (Courtesy of National Park Service.)

The forces of nature are displayed in this 1972 photograph of the floodwaters flowing down Shenandoah Street. The building to the right with the white wooden balcony was at the time the visitors' center. Note the loaded train cars on the Winchester & Potomac line; they were placed on top of the tracks to act as a bulwark against the flooding waters. (Courtesy of National Park Service.)

Photographed by David T. Gilbert, park employees are seen here filling sandbags during the flood of 1985 in the hopes of blocking the floodwater from damaging more buildings at the base of High Street. In advance of floods, park employees also remove all of the artifacts and exhibits from the first floors of all the buildings in Lower Town. (Courtesy of David Gilbert.)

Taken on November 6, 1985, this photograph by David Gilbert shows to the top left all the boarded window and door openings on the first floor of the first block of buildings on Shenandoah Street. As with 1972 and previous floods, note the railroad cars parked on the tracks to give the raised tracks more stability against the floodwaters. (Courtesy of David Gilbert.)

During the 1985 flood, John Brown's Fort is partially submerged. The fort was spared damage during the floods of 1924, 1936, and 1942 because it was then located on the high ground of the Storer College campus. Since its 1968 move back down to Lower Town, the fort has been flooded on four different occasions (1972, 1985, and twice in 1996). (Courtesy of David Gilbert.)

This 1985 photograph depicts the John Brown exhibit and other park buildings on the corner of Potomac and Shenandoah Streets inundated with waters during this flood. The park would not have to worry again about floods to Lower Town until the two separate floods of 1996. (Courtesy of David Gilbert.)

The last two major floods to imperil the park occurred in 1996. Depicted here are debris and flotsam about Arsenal Square. This photograph was taken after the water levels began to recede. Note the crest of the flooding around John Brown's Fort is marked by the darker-colored bricks showing on the lower half of the building. (Courtesy of National Park Service.)

This aerial photograph shows just how much of Lower Town is impacted by a major flood. This photograph depicts the flood that occurred in January 1996. Note that pretty much all of the park property seen here is partially submerged in floodwaters. Since the town seems to be hit with a major flood every decade or two, one wonders when the next major flood will strike the town. It has been almost 25 years since the last major flood. It was a paradox of transportation in 1747 and it is a paradox today. In 1747, the rivers brought settlers to town. But these same rivers rushed away homes and livelihoods in 1748, 1753, 1852, 1870, 1877, 1889, 1924, 1936, 1942, 1972, 1985, and twice in 1996. (Courtesy of National Park Service.)

Seven

PEOPLE OVER TIME IN HARPERS FERRY

Of course, people have been coming to Harpers Ferry for hundreds and hundreds of years. However, the park in Harpers Ferry has brought millions upon millions of people to visit the area since 1944. This 1970s photograph shows park employees who were daily engaged in the craft of living history, which entails bringing history alive and making it more realistic and relatable for park visitors. (Courtesy of National Park Service.)

In an effort to make the park as realistic as possible, numerous initiatives were undertaken in the 1960s–1990s. One such initiative, started in 1973, was a horse-mounted law enforcement unit. The superintendent at the time commented that "a sharp, confident and well-trained ranger mounted on a well-groomed horse is one of the best sights in the world." (Courtesy of Jefferson County Museum.)

During this period, as seen in this 1972 photograph, park employees were directed to use horse-drawn carriages (instead of automobiles) in conducting everyday tasks around the park, like cleaning up refuse. This program, along with the mounted ranger unit, was discontinued by the end of the decade. (Courtesy of National Park Service.)

In the 1970s, the park even experimented with a full-time sewing and tailor shop, where period outfits for the interpretative history personnel could be constructed. The sewing unit, which operated in Lower Town, would also be discontinued by the early 1980s. Pictured here is the operation in its heyday. (Courtesy of National Park Service.)

Living history, or interpretative history, in the National Park Service really took hold in Harpers Ferry starting in the 1970s. Harpers Ferry was the testing ground nationally for the National Park Service in interpretation, which would allow the visitor to relate to common figures one would have seen visiting Harpers Ferry in the 1850s or 1860s. Pictured here is a young man looking very contemplatively at a living history interpreter. (Courtesy of Jefferson County Museum.)

The concept of individuals reenacting history for visitors is a practice that started at the park during the 1959 John Brown Centennial. This centennial photograph is of a couple questioning a young man dressed up in the uniform of a Union soldier. (Courtesy of National Park Service.)

During the John Brown Centennial in 1959, the capture of John Brown by the contingent of US Marines was reenacted for a crowd of several thousand people on the old Storer College campus. This 1959 photograph depicts a moment in that reenactment when injured Marines were being taken out of the makeshift John Brown's Fort. (Courtesy of National Park Service.)

During the sesquicentennial of John Brown's raid in 2009, the capture of John Brown by the contingent of US Marines was again reenacted. This time, it was in front of a crowd of 100–200 people. However, unlike the reenactment in 1959, the actual John Brown's Fort was used. Pictured here is Brown walking out of the fort a prisoner. (Author's collection.)

For decades, the park has put on wonderful living history events where park visitors get to interact with figures from history. One of the most popular annual events is Election Day, which is depicted here. Note the man at the immediate right of this photograph, who is wearing a top hat and holding what appear to be a black cloth and stick. That is Vice Pres. John Breckinridge canvassing the crowd. (Courtesy of National Park Service.)

Another event the park has offered its visitors in the last few decades is the chance to interact with reenactors portraying famous figures who really visited Harpers Ferry, such as Meriwether Lewis or John Brown. On this occasion, the visitors were treated to visits from four famous town visitors, namely (from left to right) Frederick Douglass, Abraham Lincoln, Thomas Jefferson, and George Washington. (Courtesy of National Park Service.)

The park has also upon occasion offered its visitors the chance to interact with real-life historic figures. Since becoming a national park, several sitting US presidents have visited the park, explored its exhibits, and interacted with visitors and National Park Service employees alike. Pictured here is Pres. Jimmy Carter emerging from his automobile to visit the park in 1978. (Courtesy of National Park Service.)

Noted Civil War historian Shelby Foote (second from left) talked about the history of John Brown's raid from inside John Brown's Fort. Among others listening to Shelby Foote are First Lady Rosalyn Carter and Pres. Jimmy Carter. Much later, Shelby Foote would become well known to many Americans because of his appearance in Ken Burns's documentary *The Civil War*. (Courtesy of National Park Service.)

Pres. Jimmy Carter waves to the crowd as he emerges from John Brown's Fort. First Lady Rosalyn Carter looks anxious to return to her automobile. President Carter would not be the last sitting president to visit Harpers Ferry. Often incognito and without any notification to the park, many other prominent visitors have visited Harpers Ferry over the years. (Courtesy of National Park Service.)

The other sitting US president to visit Harpers Ferry after its establishment as a national park was Pres. Bill Clinton. President Clinton and Vice Pres. Al Gore visited the park to celebrate Earth Day on April 22, 1998. Photographed by Ranger Todd Bolton, this picture shows President Clinton speaking at the confluence of the Shenandoah and Potomac Rivers, with Vice President Gore and others listening. (Courtesy of National Park Service.)

President Clinton and Vice President Gore are seen here placing stones down next to Jefferson's Rock to stabilize a pathway. In addition to the speech at the confluence and the visit to Jefferson's Rock, President Clinton and Vice President Gore also visited the John Brown Museum. (Courtesy of the William J. Clinton Presidential Library & Museum; photograph by Ralph Alswang and White House Photograph Office.)

After notifying Pres. George W. Bush that she would resign from the Supreme Court in June 2005, Justice Sandra Day O'Connor took her law clerks to Harpers Ferry and a hike up Maryland Heights. One law clerk simply remarked that "she out-hiked us." Pictured here is Justice O'Connor at another of her frequent visits to Harpers Ferry on June 25, 1991. She is located to the rear of the boat and right next to the tour guide's dog, Clara. The guide, Jim Jenkins, is at the front. (Courtesy of Jim Jenkins.)

This 1946 photograph shows Pres. Harry Truman (right) standing next to Winston Churchill, flashing his "V for Victory" sign. The special Baltimore & Ohio train took Churchill from Washington, DC, to Missouri and back. When President Truman told Churchill that the train was passing through Harpers Ferry, Churchill responded, "I know, that's where Jackson seized McClellan's stores." (Courtesy of Harry S. Truman Library & Museum; photograph by Abbie Rowe.)

Congressman John Lewis, a civil rights icon, is pictured speaking at Harpers Ferry in May 2000 in commemoration of the bicentennial of John Brown's birth. Brown was born in May 1800 in Torrington, Connecticut. Sitting to the left in this photograph is Dr. Richard Ishmael McKinney. Dr. McKinney was the first African American president of Storer College. (Courtesy of National Park Service.)

US senator Robert C. Byrd was a longtime supporter of the park and visited many times from the 1950s to the 2000s. Byrd was the longest-serving member of the Senate (1959–2010) and longest-serving member of Congress in American history, as he also served in the House of Representatives (1953–1959). In this 1982 photograph, Senator Byrd can be seen viewing the park's new exhibit about John Brown. (Courtesy of National Park Service.)

Pictured in September 1986 is First Lady Nancy Reagan giving the kickoff speech for the Whistletot Tour for the Prevention of Drug Abuse and her more famous Just Say No campaign. Nancy Reagan is standing in front of the John Brown Museum on Shenandoah Street in the park. Harpers Ferry was the first stop of this yearlong antidrug campaign tour. (Courtesy of Ronald Reagan Library.)

At its core, people do not visit the park to see politicians. In the words of one visitor who was quoted in a 1958 *National Geographic* article on Harpers Ferry, some people may come to the park to just ask the following question: "What happened here?" This 1967 photograph depicts two people getting basic information about the park at the visitors' center. (Courtesy of National Park Service.)

Some people come to the park to just walk quaint streets of a historic village and marvel at unique architecture and history. This 1958 photograph depicts a number of people walking down Marmion Row and by the Harper House. (Courtesy of National Park Service.)

Some people come to the park to hear eminent scholars who struggle with fundamental issues like how to achieve fairness and equality. In this 1996 photograph, two-time Pulitzer Prize–winning author Dr. David Levering Lewis (left) and noted teacher and historian Dr. Henry Louis Gates (right) pose with an unidentified park guest. Drs. Lewis and Gates were both speakers for a retrospective of the Niagara Movement at Harpers Ferry. (Courtesy of National Park Service.)

Some people come to the park to hear interpretative guided talks and lectures from park rangers and guides on the plethora of events that transpired at Harpers Ferry over the past roughly 300 years. Pictured here is a park ranger from the early 1960s giving a guided talk on the 1862 siege and capture of Harpers Ferry. (Courtesy of National Park Service.)

Some people come to the park to enjoy great music. Photographed here by Ranger Todd Bolton is Benny Powell from the Don Redman Orchestra playing trombone in a concert on the old Storer College grounds. Don Redman, known as the "Little Giant of Jazz," was a Storer College graduate, and a concert named in his honor is performed every summer on the grounds of his old college. (Courtesy of National Park Service.)

Some people come to the park to participate in living history and reenactments. Pictured here are individuals reenacting a Union cavalry unit galloping through town. Note the man dressed like Santa Claus in the gap in between the four horses. That man is reenacting a Civil War–era Santa Claus for Old Tyme Christmas, which has been held every year for the last half-century. (Courtesy of National Park Service.)

Some people come to the park to connect with their past. Pictured here is the grandson of Henry T. McDonald (second from right) along with the author (second from left). The McDonald descendants came to the park to celebrate the 150th anniversary of the founding of Storer College in 1867 and were presented a gift from the author. (Author's collection.)

Some people come to Harpers Ferry to paint, write poetry, or otherwise express their artistic talents. In this 1950s photograph, two gentlemen are seated on the sidewalk and painting. (Courtesy of National Park Service.)

Some people come to Harpers Ferry to learn from history and hear from the actual participants of great events. Dr. Richard McKinney, the first African American president of Storer College, came back to the college campus in 2000 to share his recollections with the community and park visitors. Dr. McKinney (left) shakes the hand of a young student, while longtime park ranger Gwenny Roper (second from left) looks on. (Courtesy of National Park Service.)

Some people come to Harpers Ferry to be inspired by gifted individuals. Shown here is a talented park ranger talking to a group of visitors. Rangers present the history of the park that is relatable to the visitors. Visitors often leave the park wondering questions like "what would I have done if insurrection occurred in my town?" or "Is violence and law-breaking ever justified, regardless of goals?" (Courtesy of National Park Service.)

Some people come to Harpers Ferry to learn about the shared history of all Americans. Donzaleigh Abernathy (pictured here) performs a dramatic presentation on the Women of Niagara. Behind and to the left of the speaker is a picture of Dr. W.E.B. Du Bois. (Courtesy of National Park Service.)

Ultimately, the park and its resources should challenge its visitors on the many issues and dilemmas of national import that played out in Harpers Ferry over time. The children in this 1965 photograph are now grown to adulthood and may have passed on some of lessons learned at Harpers Ferry to their children, family members, or friends. Many people who visited the park as children or young adults come back to the park later in life with their children. As William Faulkner once argued, history is not the study of "was," but rather is the study of "is." That is, history and what occurred at Harpers Ferry are ultimately as much about the study of the present as the past. It should inform us all on how best to navigate life, hopefully making the country and the world a better place in the process. (Courtesy of the National Park Service.)

Visit us at
arcadiapublishing.com

CPSIA information can be obtained
at www.ICGtesting.com
Printed in the USA
BVHW021420020921
615899BV00005B/176